monographs on the ancient near east

volume 2, fascicle 3

studies in babylonian feudalism

of the kassite period

by

kemal balkan

translation by b. foster and d. gutas
introduction by b. foster

undena publications

malibu 1986

A Publication of
IIMAS
International Institute for Mesopotamian Area Studies

SOURCES AND MONOGRAPHS ON THE ANCIENT NEAR EAST

Editors: Giorgio Buccellati, Marilyn Kelly-Buccellati
Assistant Editor: Patricia Oliansky

These two series make available original documents in English translation (Sources) and important studies by modern scholars (Monographs) as a contribution to the study of the history, religion, literature, art, and archaeology of the Ancient Near East. Inexpensive and flexible in format, they are meant to serve the specialist by bringing within easy reach basic publications, often in updated versions, to provide imaginative education outlets for undergraduate and graduate courses, and to reach interested segments of the educated lay audience.

MANE 2/3

Studies in Babylonian Feudalism of the Kassite Period,
by Kemal Balkan

Translation by B. Foster and D. Gutas; Introduction by B. Foster

Kemal Balkan's "Studies in Babylonian Feudalism of the Kassite Period," a summary by the author of his doctoral dissertation written under the direction of Benno Landsberger, is here translated in full for the first time from the original Turkish. Balkan's researches on the formation and structure of Babylonian society during the second half of the second millennium B.C. should prove of interest both to specialists in Mesopotamian civilization and to historians concerned with Western Asia in the Late Bronze Age.

(c) 1986 (for English translation) by Undena Publications, P.O. Box 97, Malibu, California 90265

ISBN:0-89003-193-2

PREFACE

The basic manuscript of this translation was prepared by Benjamin R. Foster. It was then checked for accuracy by Dimitri Gutas, who made numerous corrections and improvements. The revised version was then submitted to H. G. Güterbock, who refined our rendering and offered many valuable suggestions on the basis of his intimacy with both the subject matter and the Turkish language. We would herewith express to him our warmest thanks for giving our undertaking so generously of his time and knowledge. The penultimate version was also submitted to Kemal Balkan, who read and approved it, and contributed some further suggestions, revisions, and corrections. Italicized phrases in English are Balkan's additions and show how he would emphasize the original. We are most grateful to him for his interest and support, and for his permission to republish this essay in translation. Final responsibility for errors that remain is Foster's alone.

Benjamin R. Foster
Dimitri Gutas

INTRODUCTION

Kemal Balkan's "Studies in Babylonian Feudalism of the Kassite Period"[1] is a milestone both in the development of Assyriology in Turkey and in the study of Kassite society. A summary of a doctoral dissertation written under the direction of Benno Landsberger, this essay has been hitherto most accessible from a German summary of it made by H. G. Güterbock.[2] This translation now makes available for the first time the full text of the study in English, with a few footnotes by the translator. All italics are the author's.

The non-specialist reader may wish to consider this essay against the background of three major issues. The first is the study of Kassite society itself. This began in the late nineteenth century, proceeding originally from the boundary stones, or *kudurru*s, that Balkan refers to. Beginning with a pioneering study by Cuq,[3] there developed the idea that Kassite society, especially as seen in land tenure, was "tribal" in organization. As propounded by Marxist Assyriologists in particular, this supposed tribal order was a more primitive type of land tenure and society than obtained in the preceding, Old Babylonian, period of Mesopotamian history, in which private ownership was thought to predominate.[4] The question then arose: was the alleged tribal organization of Mesopotamia under the Kassites a temporary retrogression to a more primitive type of social order, such as some Assyriologists proposed for the very earliest periods

1. "Babilde Feodalizm Araştırmaları Kas'lar Devrinde Babil," Ankara University, Dil ve Tarih–Coğrafya Fakültesi: *Dergisi* II, 1 (1943), 45-55.

2. *Archiv für Orientforschung* 15 (1945/51), 130f.

3. E. Cuq, "La propriété foncière en Chaldée d'après les pierres-limites (koudourrous) du Musée du Louvre," *Nouvelle Revue Historique du Droit Français et d'Étranger* 1906, 701-738; updated in *Études sur le droit babylonien* (Paris: 1929), 81ff. Other interpretive studies of the boundary stones, some of them later than the Kassite period, include F. X. Steinmetzer, "Über den Grundbesitz in Babylonien zur Kassitenzeit," *Der Alte Orient* 1/2 (1919); *Die babylonischen Kudurru (Grenzstein) als Urkundenform untersucht* (Paderborn, 1922); W. J. Hinke, *A New Boundary Stone of Nebuchadnezzar I from Nippur* (Philadelphia, 1907). A collection of these documents in English translation is available in L. W. King, *Babylonian Boundary Stones in the British Museum* (London, 1912). For the art, see U. Seidl, "Die babylonischen Kudurru-Reliefs." *Baghdader Mitteilungen* 4 (1968), 7-220.

4. N. M. Nikolskij, *Častnoe Zemlevladenie i Zemlepol'zovanie v drevnem Dvureč'e* (Minsk, 1948), Chapter IV, pp. 90ff. Because of the extreme rarity of this volume, it has had little impact on the field. An earlier essay by Nikolskij, "Obščina v drevnem Dvureč'e," *Vestnik Drevnej Istorii* 1938 No. 4, 72-98 deals with the question of "private" or "communal" property in early Mesopotamian history. For recent discussion of the "tribalism" question, see J. Brinkman, "The Tribal Organization of the Kassites," *Proceedings of the 27th International Congress of Orientalists* (Ann Arbor, 1967), 55f.

of Mesopotamian history, or was it an exotic, non-Mesopotamian import that came with the Kassite conquerors? Or, was tribal ownership the norm throughout Mesopotamian history and private ownership an occasional aberration? In the debate on these questions, Balkan is clearly in favor of interpreting Kassite land tenure as an import.

The second major issue is the role of temples in the economy of Mesopotamia. As noted by Balkan, early scholars of the Kassite archives, rather than of the *kudurru*s, believed that they were dealing with temple archives, and tended to posit a temple-controlled economic organization in Kassite Babylonia.[5] Balkan was one of the first to protest this interpretation of the archives.

The third issue which the reader may wish to consider is the nature of the word "feudalism" as used by historians of ancient Mesopotamia, for the word has two different senses. As some historians use the word, it is a term for an economic formation. The underlying concept had its origins in modern historical study of the Greek and Roman world that saw there capitalist formations similar to those of late nineteenth or early twentieth century Europe. Since, the view has held, the European capitalist formation was preceded by a long period of feudalism crucial to its development, so too the classical capitalist formation must have been preceded by a period of feudalism, and thereby "feudalism" has been applied to all or much of ancient Mesopotamian society.[6] As specialists within Assyriology use the term "feudalism," however, it refers to a type of economy controlled by the king who is considered "supreme owner" of all land in his kingdom and who bestows fiefs on his retainers in return for their service. In this sense "feudalism" has been widely applied to the "palace" societies of late second millennium Mesopotamia,[7] and studies of these societies have been taken as models by scholars from other fields, e.g., Mycenaean Greece.[8] The relationship of this type of feudalism to preceding and succeeding Mesopotamian historical periods is the principal difference between its use by specialists within Assyriology and its use as a blanket term for the whole of ancient Mesopotamian social history. Assyriologists debate whether or not this feudalism as they perceive it was native and typical or a foreign importation, after, as Balkan says, the "dark age." Balkan is unusual among Assyriologists in his close definition of what he understands to be feudal in Kassite society and what precisely the term feudalism means as he applies it to Kassite Babylonia.

As Balkan makes clear, the issue revolves on ownership of land, and adherents of feudal reconstructions of Mesopotamian society take as their point of departure their belief that kings were supreme owners of all land in their kingdoms. Balkan is unusual in that he faces squarely the problem of just how the king acquired this alleged supreme ownership of all land by suggesting that it was his by right of conquest. Others prefer to argue that only a defeated king's royal

---

5. For example, D. Luckenbill, "A Study of the Temple Documents from the Kassite Period," *American Journal of Semitic Languages and Literatures* 23 (1906/7), 280-322; compare also H. Torczyner, *Altbabylonische Tempelrechnungen* (Vienna, 1913).

6. For background, see for example E. Meyer, "Die wirtschaftliche Entwicklung des Altertums," *Kleine Schriften* (Halle, 1924), 1:79-168, esp. 89-98; *Geschichte des Altertums*[4] (Stuttgart, 1921), 249; F. Heichelheim, *An Ancient Economic History* (Leiden, 1965), 1:114, 167, 169. Compare, for example, T. J. Meek, *Journal of Near Eastern Studies* 5 (1946), 66 note 19, where he writes of "the feudalism of Hammurabi's time, which was manifestly very similar to that of the Middle Ages in Europe."

7. H. Lewy, "The Nuzian Feudal System," *Orientalia NS* 11 (1942), 1-40, 209-250, 297-347.

8. See M. Ventris and J. Chadwick, *Documents in Mycenaean Greek*[2] (Cambridge, 1973), 232ff., and p. 444: "It must be admitted that we committed an error in employing the word 'feudal' in our discussion of this subject [land tenure, BRF], for it has given rise to much argument and misunderstanding."

domains were a conquering king's by right of conquest, while private land remained private.[9] Thus the completeness or perfection of reconstructed feudalism depends upon how much control over land one wishes to assign the king in one's reconstruction.

A direct attack on the idea that kings were supreme owners of land in Mesopotamia has been launched by I. M. Diakonoff,[10] who asserts that such was never the case in any period, that "supreme ownership" is not only meaningless from a juridical point of view, but is also a western, medieval anachronism in a Mesopotamian context. Thus Balkan's views take their place in the midst of a lively and ongoing controversy.

Balkan's study touches on some crucial issues in interpretation of Mesopotamian society and the serious student of Mesopotamian history will want to consider his viewpoint. Of special interest is that Balkan has dealt with a group of documents not widely known among Assyriologists and hardly at all outside the discipline, and of general interest are the broader historical problems that form the background for his study and which are still far from solved.

B.R.F.

9. J. Zabločka, "Palast und König, Ein Beitrag zu den neuassyrischen Eigentumsverhältnissen," *Altorientalische Forschungen* 1 (1974), 91-114, esp. 110f.

10. I. M. Diakonoff, Problemy Ekonomiki. O strukture obščestvo bližnego vostoka do serediny II tys. do. n. è.," *Vestnik Drevnej Istorii* 1967 No. 4, 13-35. [English translation now in *Oikumene* 3 (1982), 7-32.]

STUDIES IN BABYLONIAN FEUDALISM OF THE KASSITE PERIOD

In the Near East in the first half of the sixteenth century B.C., according to the new chronology[1] of Near Eastern history, there is a period which began with the sudden silence of all the written sources at a slight interval from each other, which lasted different lengths of time in different countries, and which is known as the "Dark Age." It is an era in which happened events that left a deep impression on the history of the world. When this darkness was lifted completely from the lands of the Near East about 1400, we see the physiognomies of the states there changed radically with respect to their former conditions. The difference is to be sought in the *state organizations.* A number of tribes which had been seen at the beginning of this epoch on the fringes of this region had by now become mixed with those ruling the Near East. In fact, the *Kassites* who came from the East had taken power in Babylonia, and the Mitannians in northern Mesopotamia and Syria. Assur and Anatolia remained free from invasion.

Having in view the Babylonian, Mitannian, and Hittite states, the state organizations and administrative systems of which present a unity in essential points, as well as Assyria, which is linked with them by innumerable documents, I have undertaken to study this unity and to establish in what respects they were different from each other. I gathered the characteristics in common among these countries under the rubric *"feudalism."* I take as a working hypothesis that in all these countries new administrative systems had been established by the Kassites, Mitannians, and perhaps even the Hittites, and that the principles of large and small fiefdoms, traces of which were apparent previously, were organized on a new basis in a form most appropriate to the meaning of that concept.

Between the years 1800-1600—taking into account local differences—it is possible to find in all these countries the three basic points which belong to the concept of feudalism. We can list these as follows: 1) In all these countries the idea prevailed that the real owner of the country was *the king.* Against this right of his, private law had no validity. Landed property could be had only by grant from *the king.* At least in the beginning, one must accept that there was no land tenure outside of crown grant. 2) Between the king and the people was *a stratum of nobles.* The majority of these consisted of the royal family or of a number of persons connected with the palace. 3) Persons who had become holders of landed property were obliged to perform certain duties for the king, so that exemption was possible only by royal decree.

The investigation[2] had to begin first with Babylonia. This is because within these four

1. Balkan seems to be referring to the "Middle Chronology" of Near Eastern history, more precisely S. Smith, *Alalakh and Chronology* (London, 1940), 20ff.

2. The Turkish has Atıştırmalar "discussions," which Güterbock suggests is a misprint for Araştırmalar "studies, investigation."

states, Babylonia had the most complete organization and most extensive documentation. Furthermore, diffusion of Babylonian scribes to the countries of the Near East transported thence, even if to a slight degree, the basic forms of these institutions and the concepts belonging to them to whatever places they went. In view of this, the first necessity was to set out the Babylonian system, then, by using the results of that study as a measure, to work by comparing them to other systems and, in this fashion, to set out the peculiarities of each of the four different countries in a concrete way.

Of the four states, detailed studies of Assur, Mitanni, and Hatti have not yet been done. As for Babylonia, it has proved impossible to see truth here because people got stuck in the fixed notions that there was a temple economy and nomadic property. The Kassite epoch has entered history as a period of downfall of Babylonian culture and the Kassites as its agents. Yet in recent times this period has come to be understood as one in which *the state saw to the assemblage and protection of Babylonian literature*, in which literary works were prepared in official copies, and in which *the Akkadian language was crafted most finely*. The fact that social differentiation and state administration in Babylonia of *the Kassite period* (which we will explain below) present forms too complicated and developed to be fathomed by us has shown that this period is one of the epochs of Babylonian—and hence world—history that ought to be dwelt upon with interest.

Here I would add this about the Kassites. They came into this region from the east and settled first in the mountainous region around Suleimaniye. Their first encounters with the Babylonians occurred at the time of Hammurabi's successor.[3] Babylonian opposition having driven them west from beyond the Tigris to the middle reaches of the Euphrates, about fifty years after the Hittite campaign to Babylon they came down from the direction of this region—where they stayed but a short time—and became rulers in Babylon. Although according to Babylonian documents[4] they stayed there a period of 576 years, an important part of that figure must be assigned to the time they had not yet settled in Babylonia. *The very few words remaining of their language show that they do not belong to the Indo-Europeans*, but rather that they had been neighbors to them.

Sources. The bulk of the documents belonging to the Kassite period was found in central Babylonia at the city Nippur (present-day Nuffar) in the excavations of 1889-1900. While so far about 600 of these records, in Akkadian, have been published, the excavators said that there were more than 15,000. This does not conform, however, to the number found in museums. Of those which are not published, one part is in museums in the United States of America and most are in the Istanbul Museum. Although in the excavations attention was not paid to the find-spot of the documents, from their contents it is understood that they were an archive that belonged to the palace of the governor (**guenna**) of Nippur. Previously it was accepted that this archive was a temple archive.

The most important part of the documents are account documents concerning the administration of the province of Nippur. There is a very small number of legal documents; they are concerned with the purchase of movable property and slaves. An important part of these documents, as well, are the administrative letters. They may be divided into these main groups: 1) *royal letters.* These are a handful of short letters written by the king to the governor of Nippur province, 2) *ahu (brother) letters.* These are written to the governor of Nippur by high officials or feudal lords. In these the sender's salutation is normally "my brother" and a shortened form of

---

3. Balkan here refers to Samsuiluna, king of Babylon, who mentions a Kassite army in a year name (ca. 1740 B.C.).

4. Balkan is referring to "King List A," C. J. Gadd, *Cuneiform Texts . . . British Museum* 36, 24f.

his name, 3) *bēlu (lord) letters.* These are letters of instructions from feudal lords or high officials sent to those under their authority. 4) *ardu (slave) letters.* These were written by the addressees of the third group to their *bēlū* (lords); in these the senders call themselves the slaves of the lords. In these the salutation formula goes "My lord's house (house in the sense of fief) is well." This type contains very much information about the nature of fiefs.

If one sets aside a single letter among all these letters which may have been written to the king, one may easily understand the peculiar status held in the country by the Nippur archive, and, consequently, by the Nippur district. We also have information concerning the existence of documents written on wood which were not preserved in this archive. We should also note that the private archive of the king residing in Babylon has not yet been found.

Inscriptions found in various places in the kingdom about minor building projects and inscriptions about offerings made to the gods give almost no information at all about administration. Letters to the pharaohs of Egypt sent by the kings of Babylon found at El-Amarna in Egypt help us fill out the historical picture obtained from the Nippur documents.

An archive comprising about thirty tablets belonging to a fief holder, which comes from a city of unknown location, also has special value for our topic.[5]

The stone inscriptions called *kudurru*s (boundary stones), which belong to a later period and document land grants and exemptions, illuminate, rather than the age we are concerned with, the epoch *after* the documentation in Nippur breaks off.

The oldest document in the Nippur archives dates to the first year of Burnaburiaš II (1375). The latest dated document was written about 130 years later in the sixth year of Kaštiliaš III. This was the date of Babylon's suffering an attack by Assur, after which no document was deposited in the Nippur archive. At the same time, this event also constitutes a turning point in the feudal system.

It is understood from the examination of the documents that the administration of the Babylonian state, which presents a feudal character in the Kassite period, has to be investigated in three phases:

1. The first period (ca. 1750-1450), beginning with the settlement by the Kassites in the environs of Babylonia and the time of their coming to Babylon, and which must have reached to a time somewhat before the beginning of the Nippur archive. Concerning administration, no original document from this period remains; accordingly, we can only make inferences in this regard from documents of later periods. This was the period of establishment and development of the basic forms of feudalism. Since, in the administration of the Kassite overlords, this feudalism took the form of certain families ruling independently in the mountainous region further to the northeast, it was doubtless in the early periods very strange to the Babylonians, who were always used to centralist and bureaucratic principles. Only towards the end of this period could the Babylonian way of thinking have become familiar with this system.

2. The Classic Period of Feudalism. After the Babylonians of the first period had become acquainted with and understood overlordship, a system of overlordship emerged in which this new mentality was deftly reconciled with Babylonian traditions. Its basic forms were as follows: *A two-king administrative system* in which, along with the Kassite king of Babylon, *there was the governor of Nippur*, called the **guenna** (= **gú-en-na**), head of the Babylonian aristocrats, *in whose*

---

5. Balkan is referring to a group of documents published by F. Peiser, *Urkunden aus der Zeit der dritten babylonischen Dynastie in Urschrift, Umschrift und Übersetzung herausgegeben* (Berlin, 1905).

person there was manifested, to a certain degree, *the personality of a second king.* It was an extremely centralized overlordship which in all its economic activities was governed by the **guenna** regime in Nippur, and which can be characterized by numerous non-independent fief-lands held by Babylonians primarily in Nippur province. In this province and in other places in the kingdom were found, along with independent feudal lands belonging to Babylonians, Kassite feudatories which had been continuing from the first phase of feudalism.

May I remind the reader here that this very involved system has been portrayed until now by the simple and *entirely erroneous theory of a temple economy.* In fact, our studies have shown that the temple in this period was not the owner of landed property at all, but was provided with all its needs by the state.

3. The later *kudurru*s (boundary stones) represent another period of feudalism. In this period the **guenna** had lost his brilliant position, the central administration of Nippur disappeared, and a system of overlordship was created which could be characterized as deteriorating centralization under the government of the king.

Sketch of the Period of Classic Feudalism

The office of guenna. The word *guennakku,* borrowed into Akkadian from Sumerian, was, in the Old Babylonian period, the name of a cult place. In the Kassite period, having become the title of an office, it expressed above all the governorship of the *piḫatu* (area of responsibility in the sense of province) of Nippur. But this had come to comprise so much more power and authority that Kadašman-Enlil II assumed this title, and, when the king of Assur, Enlil-nirāri, sent a letter to a **guenna**, he called him *aḫu* (brother). These are an indication of the very highest political status of this rank. He was also at the head of the central administration run from Nippur. The authority of this governorship must have also extended to include neighboring provinces.

The **guenna**s often united in their own persons the most exalted religious office in the kingdom, that of high priest (**nu-èš**) of Enlil. A third title like **lú é-dub-ba-a** 'man of the tablet house' (Akkadian *šandabakku*), is an indication (as is evident from the meaning of the word) of their having become the highest representative of scholarship, that is, the literate arts. The **guenna** palace school was then *a university for the aristocracy of the period*, where the offspring of the king of Babylon and of the uppermost classes of neighboring countries like Elam, Arrapha, Hanigalbat, and Arabia were taught.

The Nippur documents show us an intense centralization and bureaucracy comparable only to the Sumerian administration of the Ur III dynasty. This was entirely the achievement of the **guenna**s. It is difficult to solve the problem of whether this centralization included only Nippur province or the whole country. If the second alternative is correct, determination of the real status of the king gives rise to yet another difficulty. To solve this, one may proceed from the following points: 1) Numerous letters about bringing in the harvest were constantly coming to the **guenna** from the farthest regions of the kingdom (from the coasts of the Persian Gulf, from the area around Suleimaniye, from Akkad and the regions on the borders of Elam). 2) The **guenna** is the head of the aristocrats who wrote the *aḫu* (brother) letters (see above) sent to him from various places of the country. 3) The **guenna** was the competent authority to deal with complaints coming from areas outside Nippur province. 4) The highest clerks of the central administration received orders from him. 5) In an account document, the **guenna** entered to the debit of the king debts due to the central administration for lands of the king's daughters.

On the other hand, the published texts are only a small fraction of the Nippur documents. Also, the documents written on wood which were not preserved show how rich this archive must have been. Nevertheless, that important centers of the kingdom like Babylon, Akkad, Ur, Uruk, and Dēr are mentioned in the documents only a few times or not at all does not appear to be only chance. We have already mentioned that the archive of the king was not found. Among these vexing problems, we can say confidently that at least in Nippur province there were a number of administrative units handled by the aristocrats, and that there was also a large central administration here. This was entirely the achievement of the **guenna**s, who were the heads of the Babylonian aristocratic class to which they were related.

With great difficulty we have managed to put together from the texts a nearly unbroken sequence of **guenna**s. This office must have begun a little before the Nippur archives were established. The first **guenna** we know of, Ninurta-nādin-aḫḫē, held the office from the time of Kurigalzu II to the first years of Burnaburiaš II. It is quite possible that he was not the first person to have held this office. His son Enlil-kidini succeeded him. We know this person very well from innumerable documents. He held the **guenna**-ship at the time of Burnaburiaš II and the first years of Kurigalzu III and was the most distinguished person among the holders of that office. The king of Assur, Enlil-nirāri, sent him two letters in which he addressed him informally by his name Ililiya and in one of which he called him "my brother." The succeeding **guenna**, who lived in the time of Kurigalzu and had the semi-Kassite name Nazi-Enlil, has left very few documents. His son, whose name is unknown, may have been the Ninurta-apla-iddina of the time of Nazimarutaš. Itti-Marduk-balāṭu, the protege of Kadašman-Enlil II, was probably not a **guenna**. That same king also held this title for a while. This shows the value that the kings attached to the **guenna**-ship. Amēl-Marduk, who began early in the time of Kudur-Enlil and was active throughout the reigns of Šagarakti-šuriaš and Kaštiliaš III, was the last powerful person in this position. A letter shows that he was from the family of Enlil-kidini. One can say that the **guenna**-ship was destroyed by the Assyrian invasion in the time of Kaštiliaš. After that, Enlil-zākir-šumi and Enlil-šum-imbi, whom we know from the *kudurru* of Melišipak, were, by contrast, typical of high royal officials. After the invasion, the Nippur archive suddenly falls silent. This is also an indication that the **guenna**-ship was in the process of disappearing. At that time the center of Babylonian administration must have moved from Nippur to Isin. Later still, at the time of the Babylonian invasion of Assyria and in the time of Nebuchadnezzar, only that office of the **guenna** called *šandabakku* was reinstituted as a high position.

The central administration in Nippur province. We can summarize the main lines of the very complicated central administration created by the **guenna**s as follows. The center of gravity of the relations of this system lay in the issues of land cultivation and harvesting and consumption. This process may be sketched as follows. After the state taxes were calculated, the entire harvest was delivered to state granaries. These depots, whose number was very large, were known by such names as "the storehouse" or "the encampment." All fief-holders and the people tied to them, all high officials, all temples without exception, and perhaps even the **guenna** drew all their provision needs from these depots against a receipt. Each one of these groups of people had an account in one or in a few of these depots. Subsistence rations (*epru*) for workers never exceeded a fixed amount. Shares of the higher classes (*aklu* or *ṣītu*) were not subject to such a restriction. In addition to the above, just as a distinction was made between the provisions given from these depots for external and internal expenses, there were also given from them [the depots] loans with interest (**HAR-ra**), without interest (*ḫubuttatu*), and gifts (*rimūtu*). Eighty percent of the documents filling the Nippur archives are thus accounts of deposits and distribution of this type and consist of dry, uniform, very closely written lists of names and amounts. Thanks to these and with the help, too, of the letters, we can gain insight to some extent into the administration of the fiefs of individual fief-holders and of their private households. These households are bound into an economic structure of the "closed household" type. At this point this question comes to mind: why should these fief-holders provide for these needs of theirs from the state storehouses? No complete answer can be found for this. For the present we must be content with establishing the course of the operation.

The following questions concerning operation of the storehouses remain open: we have no information on the amount given to the royal palace. The amount reserved for the **guenna**'s palace is also not all that obvious.

We have no idea about the way workmen on public works, soldiers, and militia were fed.

We do not even know where the great quantities of taxes coming from distant regions or taxes exacted from the landholders in Nippur province were disbursed.

Administrative categories of land in Babylonia. The smallest administrative unit in the country was the *ālu* (town or village; no distinction was made between town and village since *ālu* covers both). Every *ālu* was headed by a *ḫazannu* or mayor. *Ālu*s had specific territorial borders. One or more *ālu*s could be united as a fief (*bītu*). *Ālu*s were included in the following administrative units.

1) *piḫatu* = area of responsibility (in the sense of province). This was a fairly extensive administrative area composed of several *ālu*s. We can establish several such *piḫatu*s both in the classical and in the third periods of feudalism. Nippur province is one of them. In the east of Nippur between the Tigris and the mountains were Pan-ṣēri, Bīt Sin-Māgir, and Bīt Bēri. To the north, between the Tigris and the Euphrates, was the *piḫatu* of Upi. We know of several other places that we cannot locate. We have seen that the chief of the administration of Nippur province was a **guenna**. We have also mentioned (cf. p.[10]) his influence in neighboring provinces. And yet, we are not even able to say what the official capacity was of the administrative chiefs who must have headed these *piḫatu*s.

2) One category of land formed extensive, independent administrative areas under the name *mātu* = land. The area stretching from south of Nippur as far as the Persian Gulf was the *Māt Tāmti* = Sealand. In middle Babylonia there must have existed only *piḫatu*s. In the area around the center of Babylon there was *Māt Bābili*. Both of these were preserving their ancient historic names. In the northeasterly mountain region around Suleimaniye were *Māt Ḫalman* (present-day Holvan) and their neighbors *Māt Ḫamana* and *Buruttaš*. In the south toward the border of Elam was *Māt Namar*.

3) Independent *bītu*s (fiefdoms). We have mentioned that no original documents are found from the first period of feudalism. Concerning that period, we learn from the *kudurru*s (boundary stones), which are documents of the third period, and from documents from Assur of later date, that Kassite families lived in the northeast mountain region from the earliest to the latest periods. These were the areas of their main settlement before coming to Babylonia so that even after the taking of Babylon these were their centers of gravity.

These old noble Kassite families had remained there as fief-holders. For example, *Māt Namar*, on the border of Elam near the city of Dēr, was the inherited fiefdom of the Kassite family Hamban. Even after the Kassites lost control in Babylon, this fiefdom was still in the hands of that family. Concerning places like Ḫalman, Ḫamana, and Buruttaš we can scarcely think differently. *Bīt Karsiabku, Bīt Ada, Bīt Muktarissah* and *Bīt Abirattaš*, which we know of from *kudurru*s, and *Bīt Ḫašmar*, which we know of from Assyrian documents, are the oldest Kassite domains. Nearly all of them bear Kassite names and are found east of the Tigris.

Although it is certain that these were completely independent, i.e., they were not controlled by the state like the *bītu*s which we shall see in the Nippur archives, we nevertheless have no clear idea about their interrelationships with the state or the king. Nor is it clear when the founders of fiefdoms like *Bīt Sin-Māgir* and *Bīt Bēri*, which in the classical period appear like a *piḫatu*, and *Bīt Pir'-Amurru*, *Bīt Sin-šeme*, which are *piḫatu* in the *kudurru*s, and *Bīt Sin-ašarid*, were living, or when these fiefs had become provinces.

With the beginning of the Nippur archives, Babylonians also appear as fief-holders. The Babylonian noble class was gathered around the **guenna**. No mention at all is made in these documents of the Kassite lords in the east. It is possible that they were bound to the king, who was a Kassite.

We know of a good many *bītu*s in the Nippur *piḫatu* of the classic period, but they were to such an extent under the influence of the central administration that it is very difficult to follow their independent activities. We cannot as yet get to them in the real sense of the term. All the holders of *bītu*s in the Nippur area that we know of had Babylonian names. They were high officials in the central administration.

Within Nippur province the largest fief holders were the **guenna**s themselves. Of these, the Enlil-kidini family held especially vast fiefdoms in the Nippur province. From a Sumerian inscription, we learn that the first head of this family that we know of, the **guenna** Ninurta-nādin-aḫḫē, was given a plot of land by the king. From letters that came to his son, Enlil-kidini, concerning the administration of the fief, and from administrative documents, we can follow to some extent the activities and nature of the fief. For about 150 years thereafter, this fief was still in the hands of the same family. It is also established that in the north, along the Tigris, Bēl mātāti, i.e., the very extensive country thought to belong to the god Enlil, was until the latest period in the hands of this family. Males descended from this family were known as mār Enlil-kidini, i.e., sons of Enlil-kidini, for at that time *mār* PN was an expression of noble descent. We can identify in like fashion many nobles from the Nippur documents. In many instances, it is even possible to find the founders of these families who had lived decades or even centuries earlier.

There was one head of the Enlil-kidini family. But we cannot know by what rules this headship was passed on and by which way the feudal lands were parceled among the family. It is also certain that other **guenna**s were holders of comparable estates.

In the classic period we do not encounter any estate belonging to the king himself, but there are a few instances that the royal family also were fief-holders. An Amarna letter (No. 12) mentions the *bitu*s and *ālu*s of a king's son or son-in-law who went to Egypt. Among the Nippur documents there remains an account document which shows that debts of harvest deliveries due to the central administration by estates belonging to the king's daughters were transferred by the **guenna** to the debit of the king. And yet the status of the royal family is still quite unclear. This would be cleared up best of all by discovery of the king's archives.

The account lists of the Nippur archives in the classical period inform us of many individual feudal lords. These fiefs were not independent, i.e., were bound to the **guenna**'s administration. They were very possibly inherited, but this question also is still obscure. Very small fiefs are sometimes seen in the documents as *āl* PN = town of so-and-so; in such cases the fief consists of the town or village and its surroundings.

The three-generation archive of the Nabû-šarrah family, which was in the *piḫat Bīt Zazzaš* during the classic period, is an example of a non-independent *bītu* outside the province of Nippur. The members of the family were allotted shares in the fief. The head of the family would make deposits to the governor for taxes and the crown expenses (*ṣīt šarri*).

In a letter coming to Nippur from the Sea Land to the south, there is discussion of taxes of the *ālu*s, *bītu*s, *sumakti*s, and *ālik arki*s. It is certain the second of these is a fief in the sense in which we understand the term from the Nippur documents. The third and fourth were very possibly small fief-holders, but we can say nothing at all about their nature. We know only that the word *sumakti* was Kassite. These two categories were not found in Nippur. As for the first term, this was a town bound to the state and not to a fief. There is no doubt that towns of this type were found also in Nippur, even if we cannot follow the administration or identify such towns there, owing to the complexity of the central administration at Nippur. There is no indication of the existence of private ownership in Nippur outside of feudal and state ownership. There is not a single document of buying or selling of land among the limited legal documents.

The non-independent fief holders were obligated to render numerous taxes and certain services to the state. These latter were gathered under the names *ilku* and *dikūtu*. While there are few attestations in the classical period, from the succeeding period one can get a clear idea of them. It is difficult to say what *ilku* was. *Dikūtu* was certainly obligation to do labor services.

State revenues. Some tax was collected by the state from all types of land produce. Taxes were also collected for wool, hides, and oil. The taxes on grain were as follows: a) *šibšu*. This meant 1/3 of all harvests (*tēlītu*). This was an individual tax. According to the type of fief, property holders could sometimes be exempted from these. b) *miksu* was a relatively small amount. We know that exemption from this was possible by decision of the **guenna** even though it is not very clear from whom it was collected. This was also an individual tax. c) *abullu*. This tax must have been collected only from towns. To judge from its name, this was exacted from those coming to towns to do business.

In addition, there were also numerous withholdings in the form of fees for transportation, sackage, and warehousing, from people who deposited goods in central storehouses.

Classes of people. Officials: Our information concerning the palace officials of the classic period is very scanty. We cannot say what sort of official posts were held by the numerous highly placed persons about whose prosopography we have rich information. The officials who worked in the depots of the central administration receiving and issuing supplies were called "scribes" (*tupšarru*). Collection of the *miksu*-tax was done by an official called the *mākisu*. A crown official called the *rēš šarri* was concerned with inspection duties. The chief commander of the army was called by the Kassite term *sakrumaš*. Of the officials working in the closed household economies the most important were the *ābil bābi* and the *šaknu*.

Classes of people working the land: Four categories of people bound to the land have been established: a) *iššakkū ša ḫarbi*. These were cultivators bound to the plow. b) *iššakkū ša ṭēmi*. Cultivators following the command. c) *errēšū*, peasants. d) *šutapū*. Perhaps cultivators working on collective land.

Of these, the first and fourth must have had certain specified lands in a village. However, the differences among all these categories are not yet so clear as they might be. Aside from these, there were also laborers (*ṣābū*) who worked on public works projects, state lands, and waterworks.

Craftsmen. There were two types, independent and those bound to closed household economies. In the second category were all sorts of weavers, carpenters, blacksmiths, millers, brewers, oil pressers, and people in all similar professions. These worked together with all the members of their families in the mansion of the nobleman who was their boss, so that the total number of this type of workers in such a mansion would often be in the tens of people. These were called *qattinu*.

There were also a few independent craftsmen like the smith, carpenter, carter, and boatman, who performed tasks for a wage. There were also shepherds who looked after the herds of the state or *bītu*s. Although there are a few clues that there were independent people among merchants as well, we do not know whether there also were merchants of the state or of the *bītu*s.

I would like to acknowledge my debt of gratitude to my esteemed teacher Prof. Landsberger, who suggested that I study this topic whose outline I have tried to summarize, who always encouraged me through all my researches, and who was always kind enough to help with his learning in the understanding of both philological and administrative problems.

SUGGESTIONS FOR FURTHER READING

K. Balkan, *Die Sprache der Kassiten*, translated by F. R. Kraus, *American Oriental Series* 37 (New Haven, 1954). The standard study of the remains of the Kassite language.

J. Brinkman, "Kassiten" (in English), *Reallexikon der Assyriologie* 5 (1976-80), 464-473. The standard survey of what is known of the Kassites.

———, "Forced Laborers in the Middle Babylonian Period," *Journal of Cuneiform Studies* 32 (1980), 17-22.

———, "The Monarchy in the Time of the Kassite Dynasty," in P. Garelli, ed., *Le Palais et la Royauté, archéology et civilisation* (Paris: 1971), 395-408; note especially p. 406 note 83, which specifically refutes some of Balkan's theses.

E. Cassin, "Babylonien unter den Kassiten und das mittlere assyrische Reich," *Fischer Weltgeschichte* III (1966), 9-101. Interesting historical survey.

D. O. Edzard, "Die Beziehungen Babyloniens und Ägyptens in der mittelbabylonischen Zeit und das Gold," *Journal of the Economic and Social History of the Orient* 3 (1960), 38-55. Discussion of Kassite foreign relations.

M. deJ. Ellis, *Agriculture and the State in Ancient Mesopotamia, Occasional Publications of the Babylonian Fund* 1 (Philadelphia: 1976), 109ff., 150ff. Discussion of state land revenues and taxation.

K. Jaritz, "Die Kulturreste der Kassiten," *Anthropos* 55 (1960), 17-64. Survey of archeological remains that can be identified with the Kassites.

J. Oelsner, "Landvergabe im Kassitischen Babylonien," in M. A. Dandamayev et al., ed., *Societies and Languages of the Ancient Near East: Studies in Honour of I. M. Diakonoff* (Warminster 1982), 279-284.

———, "Zur Organisation des gesellschaftlichen Lebens in kassitischen und nachkassitischen Babylonien: Verwaltungsstruktur und Gemeinschaften," *Archiv für Orientforschung*, Beiheft 19 (1982), 403-410.